Salmon McCall

Culture and the Gospel

Or a Plea for the Sufficiency of the Gospel to Meet the Wants of an Enlightened Age

Salmon McCall

Culture and the Gospel
Or a Plea for the Sufficiency of the Gospel to Meet the Wants of an Enlightened Age

ISBN/EAN: 9783337252731

Printed in Europe, USA, Canada, Australia, Japan

Cover: Foto ©Lupo / pixelio.de

More available books at **www.hansebooks.com**

CULTURE AND THE GOSPEL.

Culture and the Gospel;

OR,

A PLEA

FOR

THE SUFFICIENCY OF THE GOSPEL TO MEET
THE WANTS OF AN ENLIGHTENED AGE.

By REV. S. McCALL,
OLD SAYBROOK, CT.

NEW YORK:
A. D. F. RANDOLPH AND CO.
1871.

Entered according to Act of Congress, in the year 1870, by
A. D. F. RANDOLPH AND COMPANY,
In the Office of the Librarian of Congress, at Washington.

CAMBRIDGE:
PRESS OF JOHN WILSON AND SON.

NOTE.

THE germ of this little work is a "Concio ad Clerum," preached, by appointment of the General Association of Connecticut, at New Haven, July 20, 1869, in connection with the Commencement exercises of Yale College. This may account for the particular cast of the production. The theme of that discourse was "The special adaptedness of the Gospel to the wants of an enlightened age." The discussion here takes a wider range, for the sake of more general usefulness.

CONTENTS.

CHAPTER		PAGE
I.	INTRODUCTION	1
II.	THE GOSPEL AN UNIMPEACHABLE RECORD OF FACTS	11
III.	THE DOCTRINES HIGH ENOUGH FOR THE RIPEST INTELLIGENCE	20
IV.	A RULE OF ACTION DEMANDING AND PROMOTING INTELLIGENCE	33
V.	METHOD OF OPERATION, INTELLECTUAL AND SPIRITUAL	38
VI.	THE HISTORIC DEMONSTRATION	47
VII.	AFFINITY WITH ALL TRUE CULTURE AND EXCELLENCE	52
VIII.	A CORRECTIVE OF THE FAULTS INCIDENT TO KNOWLEDGE	67
IX.	CAPABLE OF MEETING THE GROWING WANTS OF THE SOUL	75
X.	GRANDEUR OF ITS PRACTICAL MISSION	89
XI.	CONCLUSION	119

I.

INTRODUCTION.

AMONG the earliest traditions of our race is one of a golden age, when, according to the Greeks and Romans, Saturn ruled the earth. He, fearing that he should be dethroned by one of his sons, devoured his children at their birth. But Jupiter was concealed by his mother, and at an early age deposed his father, and reigned in his stead. Christianity also has its tradition of a golden age, when love reigned, and sorrow was unknown. Its records speak of the advent of a hostile power, of the entrance of Satan, sin, death, and all our woe. But they know nothing of another divinity able to wrest the sceptre from the hands of Him who first held the throne. They do not chronicle long, gloomy ages of degeneracy among men, and of strife and violence among the gods, without any promise or hope of restoration and peace. But upon the very day of Satan's first triumph came the promise of the Seed who should bruise his head. And for ages the promise was renewed, till, in the fulness of time, "God sent forth His Son, made of a woman, made under the law, to redeem them that were under the law, that we might receive the adoption of sons." The work of this Son is not to dethrone His Father, but to restore the world to its allegiance to Him; and in this restoration reproduce its golden age, with additional and higher benefits and felicities.

But there are not wanting those, who call the paradise of the Mosaic records a myth, and represent their Jehovah as an old man, too feeble to cope with the fiery genius of this age, the spirit of knowledge and wisdom and progress, the Jupiter-Tonans of the nineteenth century. They are fond of expatiating upon the antagonisms between the old Bible-religion and the discoveries of modern science, and of predicting for the latter a speedy and universal triumph. Their battle cry is, "Science must increase and prevail." But there is to us nothing terrible in that sound. We are not only quite willing that real science should increase, but we will gladly hasten its triumphs by every means at our command. We are not careful to defend any falsehood in physics, which the ignorance of any part of the church, in any age, has endorsed. The true church found out a great while ago that "the world moves." We have no controversy with real light-bearers, show us what they may.

But when men, misled by their theories and speculations, call darkness light, and parade before us "the oppositions of science falsely so called," and demand of us the surrender of our faith in the Scriptures, we are bold to tell them we prefer "the sure word of prophecy," for "the word of the Lord is tried," and we doubt not it will endure for ever. We expect science to increase, we expect progress in all departments of knowledge, we hail every indication of growing intelligence with delight. But we reserve the right to discriminate between pretenders or experimenters and real teachers.

We are aware that mistakes have been made in religion, and by religious men in matters of secular knowledge. But we think those, who have set up their theories or their discoveries against the word of God, by no means infallible. We have observed sometimes a change of base even in the so called scientific world. And even now we hear it whispered in certain quarters, with a sort of oracular assurance, that Gravitation,—which, in the hands of Newton and others, has been a golden key to unlock so many mysteries of the earth and the heavens,—is, to say the least, quite unworthy of the high honor it has enjoyed; and that a new Philosophy of Force, resolving all things into modes of motion, is the only true wisdom, and is destined to make all things new in the whole domain of human thought and knowledge. But truth is our concern, not less than it is of those, who confidently claim for themselves all the treasures of knowledge, and call us the victims of superstition. We think at least we know whom we have believed, and are ready to give an answer to every man that asketh a reason of the hope that is in us. The church having had large experience in battle with the giants, will not be dismayed by the advent of any new divinity, not even when Minerva leaps fully armed from the head of Jupiter.

It is no new thing that the preaching of the Gospel should be accounted foolishness. It was this to the cultivated men of the apostolic age. And yet it was declared to be the power and the wisdom of God, and God's foolishness to be wiser than men. In view of it, one of the loftiest intellects of that age, or of any age, indited this language: "Oh, the depth of the riches both of the wisdom and knowledge of God!" And still in view of it we may renew the challenge of the prophet, "Who hath directed the Spirit of the Lord, or being his counsellor hath taught him? With whom took he counsel, and who instructed him, and taught him in the path of judgment, and taught him knowledge, and showed to him the way of understanding?"

The Scriptures unquestionably claim for the gospel scheme the first or highest place in all the manifestations of the wisdom of God. And the writers of this book were not ignorant of the fact, that His perfections are notably displayed in the constitution of nature and man, and in the history of the world. The inference is plain and direct, that this scheme must be sufficient for the necessities of men up to any point of intelligence, which they can possibly attain.

The application of this scheme is made the special work of the Holy Spirit, who "searcheth all things, yea the deep things of God."

The end proposed to be answered by it is the highest to which any can aspire. Oneness in the faith, a practical knowledge of the Son of God, a perfect manhood, even the measure of the fulness of Christ, are combined by the great apostle as the grand aim and result of gospel teaching. "And he gave some, apostles; and some, prophets; and some, evangelists; and some, pastors and teachers; for the perfecting of the saints, for the work of the ministry, for the edifying of the body of Christ; till we all come in the unity of the faith, and of the knowledge of the Son of God, unto a perfect man, unto the measure of the stature of the fulness of Christ." If we desire to know what this fulness is, we may learn it from the Gospels and the Epistles. "And the Word was made flesh, and dwelt among us, and we beheld his glory, the glory as of the only begotten of the Father, full of grace and truth." "To this end was I born, and for this cause came I into the world, that I should bear witness unto the truth. Every one that is of the truth heareth my voice." "In whom are hid all the treasures of wisdom and knowledge." "Beware lest any man spoil you through philosophy and vain deceit, after the tradition of men, after the rudiments of the world and not after Christ. For in him dwelleth all the fulness of the Godhead bodily." Truth, knowledge, wisdom, in regal perfection, divine fulness, — can the most enlightened age rise above or go beyond these?

If we allow the Scriptures to make and plead their own claims, we shall without a question be brought to the conclusion that the gospel is adequate to the wants of any age, however ripe its culture, however advanced its intelligence. They contemplate no other scheme of religion, no change in substance of doctrine, for the better instruction of even the latest ages. The time of shadows has passed away, and the good things, which were to come, have come, and will abide until the end, till the revelation of the new heavens and the new earth, wherein dwelleth righteousness. This book has only anathemas for those who preach another gospel. Its last word of warning is this: "If any man shall add unto these things, God shall add unto him the plagues that are written in this book. And if any man shall take away from the words of the book of this prophecy, God shall take away his part out of the book of life, and out of the holy city, and from the things which are written in this book." Only those who reject the Scriptures, or at least deny their inspiration, can look for a more perfect scheme to meet the demands of an enlightened age. With this conclusion we who believe may for ourselves rest content, cleaving to the old gospel in its simplicity, without any misgivings, until we are discharged from our earthly ministry, resting upon it all our hope of personal salvation, and the completed redemption of the world.

But for the sake of those, who question the authority of this book, and more especially of those, who are in danger of being drawn away from the faith by their pretensions to a more perfect wisdom, we may be justified in setting forth some of the grounds *in reason* which support the position assumed by the Scriptures. Anything like a complete exhibition of these must take notice of the following points: A record of facts, which will bear the most rigid criticism; a system of doctrines, at least up to the level of the ripest intelligence; a rule of action, demanding the exercise of an enlightened judgment for its most perfect application; an intellectual and spiritual, rather than a physical or a sensuous, method of operation; a history, demonstrating the practical superiority of the scheme; affinity with all true culture and excellence; an efficient corrective of the faults specially developed in an advanced state of intelligence; capability of meeting the growing wants of the soul; a mission to develop and engross the best powers of the mind and heart.

II.

THE GOSPEL AN UNIMPEACHABLE RECORD OF FACTS.

THAT form of philosophy, called by its author and adherents the Positive — and which, in their belief, is the final form of knowledge, and destined to be the universal — makes a strenuous demand for facts. To this demand we take no exception. While we do not accept this philosophy as a whole, nor share the confidence of its adherents with respect to its general prevalence or its advantages, we concede the propriety of this demand. We have no answer but that of consent to the author of a Biographical History of Philosophy, when, in the interest of real knowledge as opposed to mere opinion, he quotes with approbation from the writings of Sir Francis Bacon, such words as these: "Men have sought to make a world from their own conceptions, and to draw from their own minds all the materials which they employed; but if instead of doing so they had consulted experience and observation, they would have had facts and not opinions to reason about, and might ultimately have arrived at the knowledge of the laws which govern the material world."

We propose to carry the demand for facts into the domain of spiritual as well as of material things. We hold that there are *facts* of a spiritual order, and that these, when properly verified, are the sure foundation of religion. The record which God has given of His Son is a record of facts; some of them, indeed, lying out of the range of our observation, but supported by appropriate evidence. The life of Jesus Christ, substantially as reported to us by the Evangelists, is a fact. It is no mythic figure, which moves before us upon their pages. The date, place, and circumstances of His birth and death can be accurately determined. It is worth while to remember, and to magnify even more than writers upon Christian Evidences have been wont to do, that his life was fully within the historic period. The record does not send us back to the dim shadows of uncertain tradition, but sets Him among men as distinctly seen as those of the last century. We have veritable history filling its place in the annals of a distant but not hidden age. This thing was not done in a corner.

And the testimony has not yet been successfully impeached, although thousands of the keenest intellects, and the most hostile hearts, have lent their energies to the task. We stand for the facts, we stand by the record, for reasons which satisfy us, which have satisfied many of the leading minds in all the Christian centuries, and which we are persuaded ought to satisfy the most advanced thinkers of this and every subsequent age. But this is not the place to give even a synopsis of those reasons. We have works on the Evidences, which have not been answered by the enemies of the cross, and we shall have other works as there may be occasion in the future conflicts of the church. If unbelief has more Goliahs to defy the armies of the living God, the church has more Davids to take off their heads. All that we ask of our adversaries is fair treatment of the evidences, a candid consideration of the facts. We hold, with Isaac Taylor, that, —

"If those modes of proceeding, which have been authenticated as good in other cases, are allowed to take effect in this case, nothing in the entire round of human belief is more infallibly sure than is Christianity, when it claims to be, — Religion given to man by God. It can be held in question only by aid of violence done to established principles of reasoning, and by contempt of the laws of evidence, which in all cases analagous to this are enforced."

"All things mundane I must regard as a troubled dream; all history must become as an incoherent myth, if it be not certain that the Christ of the Gospels is a reality, and the incidents of His life in the strictest sense historical." *

We invent nothing, we suppress nothing, we mean to pervert nothing, but take the duly authenticated record, and govern ourselves as the facts there inscribed require. If many of

* Restoration of Belief, pages 109 and 364.

them are not found elsewhere, this does not bring them justly under suspicion, but simply calls for a more careful testing of the accompanying proofs. If they are *sui generis*, so is their purpose, a purpose vast, good, and necessary enough to justify a new thing under the sun, especially since that thing had been the burden of prophecy for not less than four thousand years.

For the *quality* of these facts we ask, without hesitation, the respect and even the admiration of all thinking men. The incidents of that wonderful life are neither of doubtful propriety nor trivial purpose. The incarnation, the miraculous conception, the wonderful preservation in infancy, the ripe wisdom in childhood, the preaching, the healings, the miracles of every sort, the sufferings, the crucifixion, the resurrection, and the ascension, are not only peculiar, but also grand and inspiring realities. They constitute a career of surpassing beauty, dignity, power, and glory. Whoever admits that these are facts, must confess that there is no other such series of facts in the history of the world, nor even any series of fancies of equal elevation, in all the legends, fictions, and mythologies of men. Until one shall arise to outdo the works of Christ, and give better evidence of divine Sonship, we shall hold ourselves justified in challenging for Him the reverence and allegiance of all mankind.

The enemies of Christ understand very well the legitimate effect of the admission that the Evangelists have given us a true account of a real life. Hence the attempts of such men as Strauss, Renan, and Schenkel, to say nothing of other and earlier writers of the same general class, to divest the Gospels of their strictly historic character, and make them the creations of later rhapsodists, or a medley of fact and fiction, embellished by partizanship and superstition. The Christ of the Gospels, in the beauty of His faultless humanity and the power of His essential divinity, is too formidable for the peace of those, who will not bow down and worship Him. Their inward thought seems to be that of the chief priests and Pharisees, when they said, "If we let him *thus* alone, all men will believe on him; and the Romans shall come and take away both our place and nation." Hence one principal part of the work of the Christian advocate in our day is to maintain the historic accuracy, the integrity of the records, which detail the beginning and ending and manifold incidents of His matchless life. In the facts, accepted as facts, is the secret of that power, by which He will draw all men to himself.

In this connection, a word about the *number* of the facts may not be out of place. It must be confessed that for so wonderful a life the account is very brief. But this we are told is not for lack of materials. The extraordinary language of John is, "And there are also many other things which Jesus did, the which, if they should be written every one, I suppose that even the world itself could not contain the books that should be written." And yet three of the Gospels are occupied chiefly with the same things. Why this repetition; when there was so much material, and so little space allowed? To make us sure of the great things, rather than to gratify mere curiosity by a multiplicity of details. Children and unreflecting persons desire many or long-drawn stories. Maturer minds are satisfied with less particulars, and pass to the bearing of the facts related. To the ignorant, incidents are the chief thing: to the reflecting, the principles which they illustrate. The peculiarity of the Gospels, with respect to the number of facts related, commends them to the reflecting mind. Here is material enough to engage, not so much as to distract, attention, enough certainly for the profoundest study of any generation which has yet come upon the stage. Our great want today is not more facts, or greater facts, but a better appreciation of those in our possession. The apocryphal gospels were invented for weak and credulous minds, but they are an offence to sound intelligence. They show the craving of undisciplined minds for the marvelous, without reference to any great moral purpose to be served by it. But the influence is every way pernicious. The dictate of wisdom, the utterance of ancient days, an utterance still in honor among thinking men, is "Non multa sed multum." And this demand is exactly met by our Gospels in their present form.

III.

THE DOCTRINES HIGH ENOUGH FOR THE RIPEST INTELLIGENCE.

FACTS which mean nothing and teach nothing, if such a thing were possible, could possess but little or no interest for an enlightened mind. Scientific men are patient in observation, not so much for the sake of the things they see as for the sake of the truths which those things teach. Science is not the bare knowledge of facts, but rather of their relations and bearings. Out of their observations natural philosophers construct their system of philosophy, the orderly statement of those doctrines which they suppose their facts justify. In like manner gospel facts stand not alone, but are the foundation of a system of doctrines in religion and ethics. And of this system, disclosed in part by the teachings of Christ, and in part by those of the apostles, and other inspired men, we affirm that it is at least up to the level of the ripest intelligence to which any age or any man has yet attained. So much as this is requisite to its adaptedness to the wants of an enlightened age. We might claim for the gospel much more than this, without overstating its merits. It has depths which no man has yet fathomed. And this is a proof that it is not of man, nor by the will of man, but by the revelation of God. It is also an indication that it is for man in the fullest development of his powers. There ever has been, and we do not hesitate to say ever will be, something in it to invite further study on the part of the strongest and most accomplished minds. In this respect it agrees with the universal frame of nature. In the heights above and the depths beneath there are many things which the eye of no observer has yet seen, which the thought of no *savant* has yet reached. If the astronomer perfects his instruments, and so enlarges his field of vision, he is rewarded indeed by clearer views of familiar objects, but he discerns also in the receding distance other objects whose form he cannot determine. There is ever something beyond. And the fact, that it is thus with the most patient and far-seeing students of the gospel, indicates that it also is the production of the one infinite Mind.

But the simple fact that there are points of gospel doctrine as yet beyond the grasp of men, is not its only claim to the attention of intelligent minds. We do not hesitate to affirm that it has no points which are unworthy of their study, respect, and assent. It is the fashion of many in our times to exalt the gospel morality, while they deny what they call its dogmas. They have no patience with some of its doctrines. They would remand its teachings about sin, redemption, and eternal retribution to the faith of an ignorant and credulous age. They consider that the world has now no place for notions so monstrous. But we claim that its *doctrine* of sin is fully justified by the *developments* of sin even in this enlightened age, that its doctrine of redemption is still essential to the actual putting away of transgression, and that its doctrine of retribution is rendered the more credible by the light which science pours upon the sweep of natural law, and the consequences which wait on its violation.

The more man is magnified by the discovery of the possibilities latent within him, the greater must appear the wrong of either preventing these possibilities or perverting them to a base and destructive purpose. The more mind is developed, either in some particular line of progress or in the general elevation of its faculties, the higher is our estimate of its value, and the clearer our perception of the wrong, the guilt involved in its misuse. What we think excusable in an ignorant child we think heinous in an intelligent man. The gospel makes this distinction in the degrees of human guilt: "And the times of this ignorance God winked at; but now commandeth all men everywhere to repent." "If I had not come and spoken unto them, they had not had sin; but now they have no cloak for their sin." "And that servant, which knew his lord's will, and prepared not himself, neither did according to his will, shall be beaten with many stripes. But he that knew not, and did commit things worthy of stripes, shall be beaten with few stripes. For unto whomsoever much is given, of him shall much be required; and to whom men have committed much, of him they will ask the more." According to these representations, the measure of a man's guilt is determined by the measure of his light or his intelligence. No sane man can think of taking exception to this.

But the rock of offence is the tremendous consequence, which the gospel ascribes to the intelligent violation of the moral law. Many, who claim to be among the wisest of their generation, call this a horrid phantom, devised to frighten the ignorant and superstitious. But increased reflection upon the capabilities of mind, the goodness of God, the nature of moral action and moral government, and the consequences which naturally flow from transgression, ought to produce a profounder impression of the evil of sin. A perfect understanding of its relations and bearings, of the authority which it contemns, of the goodness which it wrongs, of the interests which it destroys, of the blessedness which it prevents and of the misery which it procures, of its tendency to spread its poison and perpetuate its power, would give a view of its enormity not less distinct and fearful than that which confronts us upon the sacred page. It is not the *intelligence* of men which takes offence at the gospel exhibition of human guilt. We have an *interest* in denying our guilt, or reducing it to the lowest possible point. Those who would reach a just conclusion in this matter, must let their intelligence, without their prejudices, enter into this sphere, must consent to study the deep things which pertain to this evil. A man deep in chemistry or astronomy, or in the whole round of natural science, may be profoundly ignorant here. An exclusive attention to the play of physical forces may even disqualify a man to speak of a thing so diverse in its nature as the voluntary and perverse action of a knowing mind.

And let not those who think they have disproved the existence of mind as a thing radically different from the material organism, and thereby made sin impossible, suppose that they have introduced an improvement into the economy of human thought and life. If it be so that man is doomed, by the irresistible action of physical forces, to do and continue to do, and to increase in doing, that dreadful thing which we call sin — a thing terrible in its direct influence upon others, and its reflex influence upon himself — what is he the better? If he can neither cease from it nor escape from its effects, is he not in a far worse condition than he is put by the gospel? What do we gain to be without sin, if we cannot be without this awful curse? And what claim to superior intelligence can that man have, who divests himself of the faculties and prerogatives which are the prime condition of all intelligence, who in his admiration of chemical affinities and modes of motion discrowns himself, and makes all thinking beings the slaves of a substance without the power of thought, and a process without the shadow of a purpose? Let men use their intelligence honestly and faithfully in trying to discover what they are, what is the nature and extent of their moral relations, then they will have no difficulty in seeing that sin is exceeding sinful.

Even those who cannot abide the gospel doctrine of sin, often show, by the maledictions which they pour upon its advocates, that they believe there is a thing in men bad enough to be called by the hardest names they can find or invent. To this conviction of the enormity of sin did Theodore Parker unwittingly testify, when, with a disgust and bitterness quite inexpressible, he denounced the "Christian doctrine of sin as the devil's own," and said, "I hate it, — hate it utterly."

The *developments* of sin in this day of light are so obvious, that there is no occasion for special remark concerning them in this connection.

The gospel doctrine of sin naturally carries

with it the doctrine of retribution. So great a wrong and evil deserves corresponding treatment. When we know what sin is, we are prepared to read, "The wages of sin is death." "Tribulation and anguish upon every soul of man that doeth evil." "These shall go away into everlasting punishment." And this verdict of the gospel is confirmed by the discoveries made in the domain of nature. Not only is the sweep of penalty here often tremendous and remediless, but the operation of the destructive force is secret and mysterious. The blow comes without warning, and from a quarter where no danger was suspected. And when its work is finished, neither the beginning nor the method can be discovered. When the worshippers of nature have explained these mysteries, it will be soon enough for them to cry out against the retribution of the gospel as an offence to their enlightenment. Greater things ought to be expected in the domain of the moral and the spiritual.

In keeping with the gospel doctrines of sin and retribution is its doctrine of redemption.

Nothing less than a divine Saviour can answer the cry of a soul burdened with the intelligent conviction of sin, nothing less than expiation by the blood of His cross can quell the fears of a soul looking for the due reward of its deeds. The conceit that sin may be forgiven without an atonement is a shallow thought; it comes not of deep views of moral government, or the demands and working of the human conscience. The more men see of their own needs, the more do they admire the way of salvation through Jesus Christ. And it becomes men, wise in their own esteem, to beware how they undervalue the wisdom of that scheme which angels desire to look into. Vicarious sacrifice is not a heathen conception, nor the clumsy expedient of a rude age, but God's own method for the vindication of His authority, and the deliverance of men from the curse of His law. "Other foundation can no man lay than that is laid, which is Jesus Christ." And other foundation can no man have occasion to use, however vast his knowledge, or fearful his consciousness of guilt.

The gospel furnishes the true and the only true philosophy of existence. The great and dark problems, which have in all ages perplexed the minds of men, find their solution here. Not refinements of speculation, but solid answers to the cry of the soul for light upon the end of its existence, its destiny, and the reasons of the changes which pass over it, are here furnished. Comte may declare that "human knowledge is the result of the study of the forces belonging to matter, and of the conditions or laws governing those forces." "The fundamental character of positive philosophy is, that it regards all phenomena as subjected to invariable natural laws, and considers as absolutely inaccessible to us, and as having no sense for us, every inquiry into what is termed either primary or final causes." And George Henry Lewes, sitting at his feet, and extolling him as the wisest teacher of time, may affirm that philosophy in any other sense is impossible; that men, if they travel out of this course, are doomed ever to come back to the point from whence they started. But we must think there was riper thought, as well as higher wisdom, in the answer of Schelling in his old age to one who asked him, "What is the principle and, so to speak, the key-note of the harmony of revelation with philosophy?" His reply was in the words of the great apostle: "For of Him, and through Him, and to Him, are all things, to whom be glory for ever. Amen." Then he added: "There is the foundation and the last word of philosophy."

How long will those who aspire to be philosophers, in the highest sense, continue to repeat the exploded error of astronomers in adhering to the geocentric theory of the universe? How long will they refuse to know that the true philosophy of the world, mentally and morally considered, has its centre in Christ? His appearing in our world was not an accident of that day, but the manifestation of the great purpose for which the world was made. His life was the *ruling* period of time. Philosophy will never be complete, never make legitimate progress, except as it is pursued from this centre, and under the influence of this truth. Any philosophy, worthy of the name, must recognize and duly honor "God manifest in the flesh," the grand central Power which in every age shapes the course of history.

IV.

A RULE OF ACTION DEMANDING AND PROMOTING INTELLIGENCE.

THE great principles of moral action set forth in the gospel are unchangeable. But the mode and measure of their application, in particular cases, is left very much to our individual judgment. Love to God and men embraces the whole compass of our duties. But in what ways this love shall be expressed is not prescribed, except in a few leading particulars. Prayer is one prescribed method of honoring God. And some models of prayer are furnished. But we are not shut up to the use of these models. We may frame our own speech, and ask for such things as we judge most suitable to our circumstances. We are required to remember the sabbath-day and keep it holy. But what specific actions are to be done on that day we must judge for ourselves, in view of the end to be answered and the facilities provided. We must love our neighbors as ourselves. But to which of them we should give money or other aid, and to what extent, we must decide for ourselves, in view of their necessities and our ability. It is taken for granted that the right principle in the heart, and the proper use of the intelligence, bestowed or acquired, together with such increase of wisdom as may be obtained in answer to prayer, may be safely trusted to regulate these details of daily duty.

And we can but mark a great difference in this regard between the earlier and the later prescriptions of Holy Writ. The Mosaic institutes abound in minute specifications. They fixed the place of worship, the time, order, and amount of the daily offerings. They named the precise penalty for a great number of transgressions. That mode of procedure was fitted for days of comparative ignorance and dependence. The church was then in the condition of a child, who "is under tutors and governors until the time appointed of the father." But when that first covenant, not faultless, passed away, the child was advanced from the condition of a servant to that of a son. The yoke of ceremonial prescription was taken off, and principles implanted in the heart were left comparatively free to work themselves out in such details as might best serve their great purpose. Our Saviour claimed to be Lord of the sabbath-day, and He did not scruple to do some things, and permit His disciples to do some things, which offended the strict legalists of His day. He taught that the new wine must not be put into the old bottles.

Now this gospel liberty, this flexible rule of action, — flexible not in principle, but in the application according to the exigencies of each case as apprehended by the best wisdom of the agent, — commends itself to the intelligence of mankind. It stimulates our self-respect. It gives us credit for knowing something, of being able of ourselves, in one sense, to judge what is right. We are thus treated not as children in understanding but as men. And the necessity of determining the bounds and steps of our duty, in many things, requires of us careful study, the most earnest exercise of our intelligence. It may be a convenience for an ignorant man to have a fixed rate of his duties, to be told just what and how many prayers to repeat, and just how much money to spend for religion and charity. But it may be safely asserted that such a man will remain ignorant, or make but slow progress in knowledge. The gospel is a fountain of light, and he who receives it in spirit and in truth becomes qualified for judging of his duty, as otherwise he could not be. "He that is spiritual discerneth all things." "The commandment of the Lord is pure, enlightening the eyes."

And if it be objected that with such a rule of action, throwing us so often upon our own judgment, and demanding our most careful thought to give it the best application, the uninstructed must often fall into great and disastrous errors, we may reply in the words of the apostle: "If there first be a willing mind, it is accepted according to what a man hath, and not according to that he hath not." And we may further say, that the mistakes which a conscientious man makes in trying to find out his duty are not the least valuable part of his education. And one who distrusts his own competence to judge, will not ordinarily hesitate to ask the advice of those better informed. And never, if he is sincerely desirous of knowing his duty, will he fail to "ask wisdom of God, who giveth unto all men liberally, and upbraideth not; and it shall be given him." It is taken for granted, that those who receive the gospel will not remain willingly ignorant, but search the Scriptures, and use all available means for understanding the way of the Lord more perfectly. He who is not disposed to do this, is not worthy to be called a disciple of Christ, no matter how long he may have been in communion with an organization calling itself the church of Christ.

V.

METHOD OF OPERATION, INTELLECTUAL AND SPIRITUAL.

CHRISTIANITY contemplates the growth of its adherents in every virtue, and the accession of many that are without. By what means does it aim to secure these ends? Primarily and chiefly by the preaching of the gospel. "Now after that John was put into prison, Jesus came into Galilee, preaching the gospel of the kingdom of God." "From that time Jesus began to preach, and say, Repent: for the kingdom of heaven is at hand." And when His earthly ministry was finished, He said to His disciples, "*All* power is given unto me in heaven and in earth. Go ye, therefore, and *teach* all nations, baptizing them in the name of the Father, and of the Son, and of the Holy

Ghost; *teaching* them to observe all things whatsoever I have commanded you." Immediately after His ascension, one was chosen in the place of Judas Iscariot, to be with the other apostles "a *witness* of His resurrection." When the great apostle of the Gentiles was called to his high office, and sent "to open their eyes and turn them from darkness unto light," he "*showed* first unto them of Damascus, and at Jerusalem, and throughout all the coasts of Judea, and then to the Gentiles, that they should repent and turn to God, and do works meet for repentance." Twenty-five years later, it was his joy to remember and assert that, from Jerusalem and round about unto Illyricum, he had fully *preached the gospel* of Christ." To the Corinthians he wrote, "Christ sent me not to baptize, but to preach the gospel." Here is his estimate of rites, even those of Christ's appointing, in comparison with the preaching of the gospel. Of arts and tricks to impose upon the credulity of men he knew nothing, but to despise and abhor. "We have renounced the hidden things of dishonesty, not walking in craftiness, nor handling the word of God deceitfully; but by manifestation of the truth, commending ourselves to every man's conscience in the sight of God." Miracles were to some extent also employed in those days. But the object of these was to prepare the way for the reception of the gospel. And when any required miracles, merely for the gratification of an idle curiosity, they were denied. And after Christianity was established miracles ceased. Men were then shut up to the preaching of the gospel, and the two simple rites which Christ ordained, — Baptism and the Lord's Supper.

But many who professed conversion, did not long remain content with these simple means of instruction and edification. The ordinances were grossly perverted, and to them was ascribed a regenerating power. Other rites, and ceremonies without end, were added, to dazzle the senses and charm the taste of unreflecting and unrenewed men. Thus the number of nominal adherents was rapidly multiplied. And by and by the preaching of the gospel ceased. Then the dark ages came in, and hung their pall of death over the nations. Force also became a favorite instrument for effecting conversions and preventing apostasy. The sword of the State was more in requisition than the sword of the Spirit. This was not according to the instructions of Christ. His way of discipling the nations was by *teaching* them, by appointing chosen men to tell them the story of the Lord, to preach among them the unsearchable riches of His wisdom, love, and grace. And since preaching has been restored to its appointed place in the Protestant church, a new era for the intelligence of mankind has opened upon the world.

One still standing among us has paid a fitting tribute to the intelligence of an earlier generation in our Commonwealth, whom he represents as content to sit without fire, in an open house, long hours in the drear winter time, listening to the word of life. His words are: "There is no affectation of seriousness in the assembly, no mannerism of worship; some would say too little of the manner of worship. They think of nothing, in fact, save what meets their intelligence, and enters into them by that method. They appear like men, who have a digestion for strong meat, and have no conception that trifles more delicate can be of any account to feed the system. . . . Under their hard and, as some would say, stolid faces, great thoughts are brewing, and these keep them warm. Free-will, fixed fate, foreknowledge absolute, trinity, redemption, special grace, — give them any thing high enough, and the tough muscle of their inward man will be climbing sturdily into it; and if they go away having something to think of, they have had a good day. A perceptible glow will kindle in their hard faces, only when some one of the chief apostles — a Day, a Smith, or a Bellamy — has come to lead them up some higher pinnacle of thought, or pile upon their sturdy mind some heavier weight of argument."

A noble generation of men, and worthily commended to the study and imitation of these softer and more graceful days. Would that an intelligence not less sturdy, in spiritual things, were blended with the refinements of this age. Is there not in many places occasion for the rebuke administered to the Hebrews? "When for the time ye ought to be teachers, ye have need that one teach you again which be the first principles of the oracles of God, and are become such as have need of milk and not of strong meat." Is not this the explanation of the recent rapid growth of ritualism?

It is true, historically, that ritualism has flourished greatly in times of general ignorance. A barbarous people can appreciate its gorgeous displays. And the low degree of general culture among the chosen people may be one principal reason why the appointments for the tabernacle and temple were so magnificent. A further reason may have been, to show the world the unsatisfying nature of the experiment. It is quite certain that, in the early days of Christianity, no account was made of such things. They were not only not relied upon, but they were discarded. Christ took upon Himself the form of a servant, and made Himself of no reputation. He would not be made a king. The first disciples and apostles were plain fishermen. The great apostle shunned the brilliant rhetoric of his day. But if Christianity ever needed the aid of an imposing ceremonial, it was at the outset. But then it was utterly rejected, and it ought to be discarded to the end of the world. Let it be attached to false religions that have nothing else to recommend them to the acceptance of mankind, or be remembered as an adjunct of an imperfect system, which God meant only for the childhood of the race. adopted as a temporary and preparatory expedient until the times of the reformation. The modern apostles of ritualism offer an affront to the intelligence of this age, while they obscure the glory of the cross. The gospel asks no such service at their hands, while discerning minds reject it as a degradation of the religion it professes to honor, and a fearful wrong to the souls it attempts to guide. God's truth shines by its own supernal brightness, for low and high, for the ignorant and the learned, "the light of the knowledge of the glory of God in the face of

Jesus Christ." It asks not the poor candles of human invention to help it irradiate the world. Away with these rush-lights, these robes curiously wrought, these censers and processions, away with every thing which comes between the simple truth of the gospel and the minds and hearts of men, who must be saved by the intelligent apprehension and the hearty reception of it, or be lost for ever. Christianity has indeed its symbolism, but it is the very essence of simplicity and transparency,—water for baptism into the name of Father, Son, and Holy Ghost; bread and wine for showing forth the Lord's death until He comes; the word of truth for correction and instruction in righteousness. These address directly and powerfully the intelligence of men.

But the gospel method of operation is not of the intellectual order only. It is also spiritual. The gospel does indeed invite and demand the thoughtful attention, the candid, earnest, persistent consideration of men, but it does not rest upon this method alone. In fact no vital change is expected without the power of the

Holy Ghost. It is most agreeable to reason that He, who made the mind, should have full access to it, and know how to work changes in it. And according to the Scriptures, the most radical change which is ever made in it, is wrought by the Holy Spirit. He who created can renew. But this renewal, by a special exercise of divine power, is not independent of the truth. The sword of the Spirit is the word of God. The heirs of eternal life are chosen to salvation through sanctification of the Spirit and belief of the truth. It was when the apostles preached, that the Holy Ghost fell on them which heard the word. This combined power of the word, and the Inspirer of the word, must not only be the most efficient possible, but also commend itself to the reflecting mind as the most fit and worthy agency for reaching and transforming, for enlightening, subduing, elevating, and perfecting men.

VI.

THE HISTORIC DEMONSTRATION.

IT surely is reasonable to ask that, in the course of eighteen centuries, the gospel should accomplish something worthy of its claims. The time has been long enough for a conclusive demonstration. And this we hold has been given. We freely admit that, as yet, it has gained the adhesion of only a fraction of the race. But the explanation of this fact is found in the nature of its appeal. It does not come upon men with an overwhelming force, but comes to them with considerations of reason and truth, with motives which they may either receive or reject. They may even resist the Holy Ghost, and He will leave them to their own chosen ways. The native bias of the heart is opposed to the gospel. All the progress it has made in the world has been in the way of conquest, overcoming that toughest of all resistants, human depravity. If men, or generations, in the pride of their self-will, and the love of sinful pleasures, would none of it, so much the worse for them; but this detracts nothing from its inherent worth. If God, in view of their perversity, gave them over to a reprobate mind, this is no impeachment of His goodness, and their doom is no reflection upon the grace which would have saved them, if they would have received it. This grace would be infinitely glorious if all men should reject it.

And yet, as a practical scheme of redemption, the gospel must be declared a failure, unless it can be shown that it has won many and substantial triumphs. A vast multitude have embraced it, and given the highest possible evidence of their sincerity in so doing. The Acts of the Apostles herald its early victories. And they tell us what manner of men those became who received it. They continued steadfastly in the truth and worship of Christ.

and sold their possessions and goods, and parted them to all men as they had need. In later days, impurities came in to disturb the course of its history. And the written annals of the church may have preserved more of her controversies and mistakes, than of her truthful inculcations and her benefactions. But even in her worst estate, she was doing signal service for mankind. Her noble army of martys can never be forgotten. Her work, in preserving both secular and sacred learning, can hardly be too highly prized. Nations of barbarians have been tamed and civilized by the power of the cross. The habitations of cruelty have been transformed into the abodes of charity and peace. Altars wet with human blood have been thrown down, and temples consecrated to Jehovah have been reared up in their stead. Asylums for the unfortunate and the wretched have been opened in many lands. Prisons have lost their tortures, and slaves have been delivered from their fetters. Governments have learned the humanities of their office, and peoples the sacredness of their rights.

Homes and schools and churches have been made the nurseries of learning, piety, philanthropy, all the graces of refinement, all the fruits of civilization. And the blessed work wrought in individual souls cannot be named or estimated. What righteousness, what peace, what joy in the Holy Ghost! What zeal in life, what transports in a dying hour! And there is to-day a great army, toiling in patience, waiting in hope, praying in faith, looking with confidence, for the overthrow of all wickedness, and the perfect establishment of righteousness and peace in all the earth. It were easy to speak of wrongs in the past and defects in the present. But in spite of these, we maintain that the adherents of the gospel, the true disciples of Christ, as a body, are in the van of all movements calculated to restore man to himself, his true place in society, and his allegiance to God. Others may be more boastful in pretensions, more extreme in expedients, more fierce in invectives, more violent in demonstrations, but the great burden of the real work of renewing the face of the earth rests upon the shoulders of the army enlisted under Christ. The path of the gospel through the ages has been a track of light, and notwithstanding all the errors and impurities and wrongs which have taken shelter under the name of the church, and all the prejudice raised thereby against the cause of Christ, we believe that it will lead right on and upward, till He shall be enthroned over the nations, and all nations shall be blessed in Him.

VII.

AFFINITY WITH ALL TRUE CULTURE AND EXCELLENCE.

IT has not been uncommon to represent Christianity as hostile to many other forms of the good, the true, and the beautiful. And occasion has been found in the manner in which some Christians have spoken of and treated these things. They may have erred, but it is quite as likely that they have been misunderstood. It is common for evangelical preachers to speak of the total depravity of unrenewed men, notwithstanding all the pleasing and commendable traits which they may possess. This sort of language does not deny that for some purposes the natural virtues, as they are called, are good and useful. But it declares that in the matter of justification before

God they are of no account whatever, inasmuch as the radical principle of action is utterly wanting in that regard for God and His will and glory, which is the very essence of holiness. Repentance toward God, and faith in our Lord Jesus Christ, are insisted upon first of all, not as arbitrary terms of salvation, but as involving the new and holy principle from which right actions will proceed. None can be more earnest than the preachers of total depravity, in exhorting believers to "maintain good works for necessary uses." If Luther was afraid of the Epistle of James, because he read in it, "Ye see then how that by works a man is justified, and not by faith only," this must be put to the account of his want of completeness in the knowledge of God, a want which can surprise no man, who thoughtfully considers the errors of doctrine and practice so rife in his day. It is rather to be wondered at that he came so near complete emancipation from the falsehoods and abuses in which he was trained. Good works, in their proper place, cannot well be magnified more than they are in the gospel, while it does not ascribe to them an importance in other relations, which must utterly disappoint those who trust in them.

It is common for a certain class of writers and speakers to declaim against the church as a stickler for dead dogmas, but indifferent to the great practical issues of the day. To this accusation we have three replies. First, for the most part it is false. In the main, the church — the living, evangelical church — is, to say the least, abreast of any other body of progressive men in matters of reform. In some matters of innovation, which are not of reform, the church is quite willing that others should do the work and reap the reward. When it comes to giving and doing and suffering and dying for a worthy object, the hosts of the church will not be found wanting, as compared with any other body of men. So long as there is nothing but *speaking* to be done, other voices may perhaps be louder than hers.

Our second reply is, that the church has always in hand a greater work than what are called the issues of the day. In her view, to save a soul from death, and hide a multitude of sins, is greater than to save a kingdom from anarchy or despotism; to put a man in the way to heaven, is better than to lavish upon him all the treasures of wealth and liberty and learning. First, the kingdom of God and His righteousness; then all other good things as there may be opportunity for gaining and using them consistently with the great commanding purpose.

Our third answer is, that the fundamental work of the church is the most reliable support, the most efficient promoter, of every good thing in man and in society. Regenerated men are the best material and the best instruments for any great undertaking, or for any worthy enterprise that is not great, — whether you would build a character, a home, a literature, or a nation. First, get the man right in his views of the great end of life, in his spirit, in his feeling of brotherhood with all the race, in his consciousness of fellowship with God, — then will his own invigorated faculties find out a way of rendering service to his kind; then will his own ever-gushing impulses urge him onward in a career of self-denial, toil, endurance, honor, usefulness. He is *fit* for a friend, a neighbor, a citizen, a philanthropist. He will build on the everlasting foundations, and his work in substance shall abide, no matter how many nor what sort of revolutions may assail it. The form only can ever pass away. With very defective political and social institutions, he will do better for himself and for humanity than one, who knows nothing of true gospel power, in his own experience, can possibly do with the most perfect organizations; and at the same time, he will make sure and steady progress toward the reformation of those faulty institutions.

Follow the missionary of the Cross from his Christian home to his chosen field of self-denial among the heathen. Mark the despotism, the ignorance, the superstition, the degradation, the barbarism, which confront him at every step. Tarry with him till he grows old in the service, and forgets his mother tongue. Observe now the change in his field of labor.

The government has learned to respect the rights of conscience. The people have become industrious and moral. The idol shrines are forsaken. The house of God is filled with reverent worshippers. Falsehood, theft, violence, have disappeared. Charity, with open hand, feeds the hungry, relieves the distressed. The solitary place is glad, the desert blossoms as the rose. This is gospel work, the work of men who hold, and who find all their inspiration in, the grand old doctrines which some are pleased to call the antiquated rubbish of a metaphysical or controversial, not a practical age.

But we must pass on to look at this matter in other relations. *Liberty* has been regarded among enlightened nations as one of the greatest blessings. With the progress of light in this century, the cry for liberty has waxed louder and louder. Even old Spain, the home of the Inquisition, is beginning to hear the cry, and to feel the stirring of a new life in her darkened soul. Is the gospel unfriendly to this cry? Not unless it means liberty to blaspheme the name of God, and wage war upon the dearest rights of mankind. Christ, at the very outset, proclaimed deliverance to the captives, and liberty to them that are bruised. The great apostle speaks of the glorious liberty of the children of God. Where does liberty dispense its choicest blessings to-day? In England, Scotland, and these United States, the most nearly Christian countries in the world, the lands in which true gospel preaching has most place and power. Guizot affirms that the comparative histories of the world, whether Christian or Pagan, place it beyond all doubt "that Christianity alone restored to man, as man, and for no other reason, his rights to liberty." And Farrar, in his "History of Free Thought," declares that it was Milton, that prince of Christian poets and writers upon civil affairs, "who first enunciated in its breadth the principle of universal religious freedom and liberty of conscience."

The *love of the beautiful* is characteristic of an enlightened age or people. Does the gospel encourage or repress it? Had we space we might pursue this inquiry with reference to architecture, sculpture, painting, poetry, music, oratory, and general refinement or elegance in the business, courtesies, and enjoyments of life. But a particular examination of this wide and inviting field is obviously quite impracticable in this connection. There is material here for a volume, by which some true disciple of Christ and true lover of Art may instruct and enrich his generation. There is room in this place for nothing more than the statement and brief defence of the doctrine in general, that *the gospel favors all these so far as it may without detriment to its grand purpose* — the *regeneration* of the world, the *salvation* of the soul.

True gospel work is a *refining* process. Its aim is perfect moral excellence. Its legitimate effect in all other relations must be in keeping with this. If the effect is ever otherwise, it must be ascribed to an alien element, which has come in to disturb the normal action of the gospel. It cannot, however, be denied that those bearing the name of Christ have sometimes manifested indifference, or even hostility, to the creations of Art. It is freely allowed that the appearance of Christ, and the style of the great apostle, did not indicate any ambition for artistic perfection. And some may recall the words of Peter: "Whose adorning, let it not be that outward adorning of plaiting the hair, and of wearing of gold, or of putting on apparel, but let it be the hidden man of the heart, in that which is not corruptible, even the ornament of a meek and quiet spirit, which is in the sight of God of great price." Not a few passages of like tenor may be gathered out of the word of God. In explanation of these things two points are to be considered, the relative importance of outward graces, and the disposition of men to magnify them unduly. As compared with the graces of the Spirit, the beauty of holiness, they are not of great account. And if the question is, Which shall be sacrificed for the other? there can be no hesitation in deciding that the less must yield to the greater. And the truth is, that men are so readily captivated by the outward and the sensuous, that it is ever necessary to guard against its encroachment upon the spiritual. If the right eye offends, it must be plucked out; the right hand be cut off. But it is only when the outward withdraws attention from the inward, only when the sensuous obscures the spiritual, that there is occasion for applying this precept of the gospel. In subordination, all these graces of form, manner, and action, may minister to the edifying of the body of Christ. But in subordination they must be kept, or put away. Whatever men can bear with safety to their spiritual integrity, progress, and usefulness, they are allowed: more than this they may not innocently desire.

It is not because these things are evil in themselves, but because we are prone to make a god of them, that we are charged to take heed lest they prove a snare to our souls. In a perfect state, there will be no need of this caution. The thoroughly sanctified spirit may go in and out among the fairest creations of even divine skill, without hindrance or abatement of its delight. The New Jerusalem, descending out of heaven from God, prepared as a bride adorned for her husband, having the glory of God, is the perfection of beauty. And this shall be the home of the ransomed for ever. To pass through its pearly gates, to gaze at its jasper walls, to tread its golden streets, to handle its harps and palms and crowns, to hear its mighty voices and its melodious songs, to be surrounded by its splendors and filled with its magnificence, shall be the portion of all who " have washed their robes, and made them white, in the blood of the Lamb." It shall be their portion, because for them it will be safe. But while we are in the flesh, we must consider what and how much we can bear without prejudice to our character, and our hope of everlasting life.

It is the thought of some that paradise restored would end our woes. But they forget that all the charms of Eden kept not sin out of the world. If the innocent fell, in the midst of all these delights, how can we think that plenty and beauty are the prime necessity of fallen and guilty men? No, the work of sin must be undone, the world renewed, before paradise can be safely restored. As the world progresses toward the sinless state, through the rectifying power of the Cross, the outward condition may, with safety, increase its charms. But while the church is in deadly conflict with the powers of darkness, all her energies should be consecrated to her work, and her appearance that of one girded for battle. It is no time to sit down and clothe herself in holiday attire, while the enemy is coming in like a flood, and souls are pressing down to death.

When our Lord began his ministry, there was no lack of outward splendor in church or state. The temple at Jerusalem was blazing with magnificence. Athens and Rome were filled with costly shrines and beautiful statues of the gods. Poetry produced the strains, and eloquence the speeches, which the world is still charmed to hear. But Jews, Greeks, Romans, and barbarians, were alike dead in trespasses and sins. Society was a garnished sepulchre. The work to be done was to strip off this covering of deceit, and create a new life in the centre of the soul. In this vital work little account could be made of ornaments, which, to say the least, would not help the great endeavor; and which, in consequence of their association with degrading mythologies and dead formalism, were likely either to obscure its purpose or corrupt its adherents. In the great crises of history men are too earnest, too much intent upon the vital issue to give much indulgence to the passion for the beautiful.

And this consideration goes far to explain the fact that, in some departments of Art, the old masters of the pagan world have never been surpassed. While we do not admit that, all things considered, there has been no progress, no development, no elevation of the artistic idea, under the reign of Christianity, we are willing to allow that in some departments, like that of sculpture for example, the ancients of the ante-Christian age came as near perfection as any of a later day. And if this be named as a reproach to the gospel, our answer is that the great concern of its true adherents has ever been not to make faultless statues, dead images, but perfect men, alive with the noblest impulses, active in the holiest ministries, adorned with the choicest graces, animated by the loftiest hopes, and sealed as the heirs of immortality. This work is immeasurably nobler than the grandest and the most finished creations or imitations of Art.

But we may claim a very high place in this matter of Art for our holy religion. Indeed, some portions of the sacred writings are of inimitable beauty and sublimity. And but for the gospel, where had been Handel's unmatched Oratorio of the Messiah, Dante's Divina Commedia, Milton's Paradise Lost, Leonardo da Vinci's Last Supper, Michael Angelo's Last Judgment, Volterra's Descent from the Cross, or Raphael's Transfiguration? However defective may have been the character of any of these, or other great masters, in Christian Art, it is undeniable that they drew their inspiration from the oracles of God. These gave them the sublime conception which, more than their style of expression, is the abiding charm of their work. Let rationalism, positivism, naturalism, do better and greater things than these, ere we are summoned to exchange our Faith for their Unbelief. In his life of Michael Angelo, Herman Grimm has recorded a fact, or uttered an opinion, which is worth the study of those who would banish the supernatural from the world. His words are: "The decline of painting and sculpture began when the sacred element wholly disappeared, and when the artist's single aim was to satisfy the purchaser of the work." Art can never do its best, both in theme and expression, until it feels the breathing of the Divine Spirit, grasps some great divine thought, and bathes itself in the radiance of the divine glory.

VIII.

A CORRECTIVE OF THE FAULTS INCIDENT TO KNOWLEDGE.

LIGHT is always good if a man will use it lawfully. But it is the prerogative of a free agent, and very often the impulse of the human agent, to use it unlawfully. No one thinks of controverting the adage, "Knowledge is power." But it must be remembered, that it is power in the bad as well as in the good. It may indeed be claimed, that the legitimate influence of knowledge is purifying and elevating; that other things being equal, crimes and gross immoralities will abound more in an ignorant than in an enlightened community. And yet it is incontrovertible, that many learned men have been also very profligate, and a greater scourge to society in consequence of their learning. And it is generally supposed that the Augustan age, eminent in letters, was among the most corrupt in Roman history. And the subsequent decay of learning was the effect more than the cause of moral degeneracy. And it is the conviction of many among us in advanced life, who can remember the two generations before them, and observe the two following them, that the moral tone of society has not, to say the least, kept pace with the increase and diffusion of knowledge. And there are not wanting those who affirm positively, that the loss in morals has been greater than the gain in learning. Considering the measure of light now enjoyed, we have certainly no occasion to boast of the moral purity and vigor of society. The frequency and enormity of crimes, the prevalence of social and vicious dissipation, to say nothing of profanity and blasphemy, forbid our glorying, lest we glory in our shame.

And, most certainly, it cannot be supposed that the gospel has contributed materially and directly to the prevalence of these abominations, for it is in continual protest against them. The explanation was long ago recorded by the prophet Isaiah: "Thy wisdom and thy knowledge it hath perverted thee, and thou hast said in thine heart, I am, and none else beside me." And to the same purpose are the words of the apostle: "Knowledge puffeth up, but charity edifieth. And if any man think that he knoweth any thing, he knoweth nothing yet as he ought to know." Does the gospel then set its face against knowledge? By no means. The same apostle, writing to the same church, used this language: "Brethren, be not children in understanding: howbeit in malice be ye children, but in understanding be men." It is the abuse of knowledge against which we are warned. If men think they have made great attainments in it, they are prone to be proud, puffed up with the conceit of their own consequence. And this pride stands in the way of further attainments, if it does not make useless or pernicious those already gained. The influence of the gospel tends to abase this pride, and keep men ever learning and ever turning their knowledge to good account.

It may indeed be said, that the more thoroughly a man is educated, the less likely is he to be proud. We freely allow it, provided his education be symmetrical, including the knowledge of God as well as the knowledge of nature, and the training of the moral as well as the intellectual part. But the question is, How to get men safely up to this point of a thorough education : how to carry them past the perils which beset them by the way, and to give them the requisite impulse to push forward to the goal. Pride is apt to spoil the work while in progress. Here is needed a sanative moral influence to humble and quicken the soul. And this is furnished by the gospel. Here we are taught the nothingness of human excellence and acquirements. Here we learn to put a true estimate, both in kind and degree, upon the treasures of human learning. We discover that the wisdom of the world is nought without the knowledge of God. We see that the grandest heights of human thought are infinitely below the thoughts of God.

If pride does not stay the march of intellect,

ambition is likely to convert it into a crusade of violence and destruction. When the progress of knowledge is rapid, great forces are developed, great schemes conceived, which will prove a bane or a blessing according to the direction which is given them. And this direction depends chiefly upon the prevailing moral tone. If this is corrupt, a fierce competition for wealth, honor, and power, will generate gigantic frauds in business and politics, unsettle the confidence of men in each other, and not unlikely desolate a continent by the sweep of war. If, on the other hand, the moral tone is pure and high, these forces will be made the instruments of a beneficent progress in the conveniences and comforts of life, in the general culture of society, and in all the arts and appliances and resources which characterize an advancing civilization. What can give the requisite moral tone but the gospel? Knowing the power of self-interest and carnal ambition, we shall stultify ourselves if we suppose that the sense of honor and self-respect, or the generous sympathies native to the human heart, will alone furnish any effectual restraint upon the lawless passions. Nothing but moral principle, born of the Divine Spirit, and supported by the high sanctions of divine revelation, can meet the emergency. In the midst of light, which shows men how to wield the arts of Satanic cunning, there must be the regenerating and sanctifying efficiency of the Holy Ghost, or society, — under the spur of a mad ambition for great things, of honor, power, gain, and pleasure, — will rush into the abyss of corruption and destruction.

If it be said that the gospel has no appreciable influence in counteracting the fierce passion for gain and self-aggrandizement, stimulated by the facilities which knowledge supplies, we answer that it has, in fact, much less than we desire, but that without it the evil would be far worse. And we further allege that, but for the teachings of unbelief, it would have far greater power. Where received, the gospel does moderate, if not destroy, the ambition to get great things for one's self. And but for those who deny its claims, it would be far more generally received. Those who would take the reins out of its hands know not what they do. Their conceit of superiority is a dangerous thing for themselves and the world. Let them increase in knowledge as rapidly as they can, but let them never suppose themselves wiser than God. It were well for them to recall the story of the Titans attempting to scale the heights of heaven, and of Phaeton to guide the chariot of the sun. It were better still for them to ponder, with a teachable mind, the inspired account of the first human pair, who, deceived by the father of lies, and aspiring to be gods in wisdom and knowledge, fell from their high estate, lost the pure image of their Creator, and let in upon themselves and the world floods of error, sin, and woe. At first, as Milton writes, —

> "As with new wine intoxicated both,
> They swim in mirth, and fancy that they feel
> Divinity within them breeding wings
> Wherewith to scorn the earth."

But at length reflection comes; they wake from their guilty dream, and seek a covering for their shame.

"They sat them down to weep; nor only tears
Rained at their eyes, but high winds worse within
Began to rise, high passions, anger, hate,
Mistrust, suspicion, discord, and shook sore
Their inward state of mind, calm region once
And full of peace, now lost and turbulent:
For understanding ruled not, and the will
Heard not her lore; both in subjection now
To sensual appetite, who from beneath
Usurping over sovereign reason claimed superior sway."

IX.

CAPABLE OF MEETING THE GROWING WANTS OF THE SOUL.

IT must not be forgotten that the more men know the more they want. Desire not only keeps pace with attainment, but goes ever beyond it, and even grows with greater rapidity. Few and simple things satisfy the desires of the savage. A rude wigwam for his dwelling, the primeval forest for his hunting ground, a little fish and maize for his food, skins for his clothing, the war dance for his amusement, and some low, vague notions of a divinity, with corresponding rites of worship for his religion, — these meet the chief part of his felt necessities. But to the man of cultivation and refinement they are as nothing, or perhaps even an offence and irritation. Better and greater things than these are required for his comfort day by day. And with all his ingenuity of invention, and facilities of communication, he cannot obtain supplies with sufficient rapidity, and in sufficient measure, to make him content. His eagerness for something new is stimulated rather than satisfied by every fresh acquisition. The thirst for knowledge increases with attainment, like the passion for gold. Larger and more refined conceptions in religion reach up for something still greater and higher.

Now the question arises, Is the soul doomed to this indefinite expansion of its desires without the possibility of finding any object vast enough to fill them, and keep them filled always and everywhere? This question must be answered in the affirmative, unless there is some Being able to do more for us than all the mythologies, the philosophies, the arts, and the sciences of men, either in their present condition or in any improved state to which the studies and labors of human genius may bring them. The universe is indeed vast, and we are yet far short of a complete knowledge of its manifold objects, processes, relations, and uses. A great measure of satisfaction is yet to be enjoyed from the discoveries which will be made. But these discoveries will develop the human soul into still grander proportions, and set it upon asking questions still more difficult to be answered. And what shall be the end? Is there no resting place for this aspiring, yearning, expanding spirit?

The gospel answers this question. It brings us to the Infinite in a personal form, and satisfying relations. This great, growing, human mind it sets face to face with the Infinite understanding, and bids it commune with the Author of its being,—bids it ask its far-reaching questions of Him who gave the power to ask, and holds the power to answer. On nothing below Him can rest the fully awakened and developed human mind. All possibilities of thought and knowledge are with Him. And He is accessible to His rational creatures. He may be known of them, and in knowing Him they may be satisfied. If they know less of Him than they desire, they may increase in that knowledge, and go on increasing for ever, and find in all increase added joy. The Father of our spirits, the God and Father of our Lord Jesus Christ, is the God of all comfort, the God of peace. To the best knowledge He adds the gifts of faith and hope.

It is matter of experience that many of the most gifted and cultured souls, reconciled to Him, resting upon Him, have found peace, even that peace which passeth all understanding. He who has found a gospel which can inspire, and a God who can answer, such a prayer as that of the great apostle for the church at Ephesus, must be satisfied, however vast and varied his desires, or however rapid the rate of their increase: "That he would grant you, according to the riches of his glory, to be strengthened with might by his Spirit in the inner man; that Christ may dwell in your hearts by faith; that ye, being rooted and grounded in love, may be able to comprehend with all saints what is the breadth, and length, and depth, and height; and to know the love of Christ, which passeth knowledge, that ye might be filled with all the fulness of God." From the ever exultant soul of such a man must break forth the doxology: "Now unto him that is able to do exceeding abundantly above all that we ask or think, according to the power that worketh in us, unto him be glory in the church by Christ Jesus throughout all ages, world without end. Amen."

The question of range, or compass of thought, is not the only one answered for the soul in the God of the gospel. The need of forgiveness is liable to be felt more and more, as the soul advances in the knowledge of God and itself. His holiness will appear more glorious, its impurity more loathsome; His authority more sacred, its sin more criminal; His displeasure more awful, its guilt more inexcusable. It is unquestionably true, in many cases at least, that the more men grow, both in knowledge and grace, the deeper is their sense of sin, the more they abhor themselves. Not sin in general alone, nor some gross forms of it observed in others, but their own heart sins take on an enormity, in their view, which is quite inexpressible. No sane man will question either the intelligence or the comparative purity of Jonathan Edwards. But this saintly man has left on record this expression of his sense of sin: "When I look into my heart, and take a view of my wickedness, it looks like an abyss infinitely deeper than hell. And it appears to me, that were it not for free grace, exalted and raised up to the infinite height of all the fulness and glory of the great Jehovah, and the arm of his power and grace stretched forth in all the majesty of his power, and in all the glory of his sovereignty, I should appear sunk down in my sins below hell itself; far beyond the sight of every thing but the eye of sovereign grace, that can pierce even down to such a depth. And yet it seems to me, that my conviction of sin is exceeding small and faint: it is enough to amaze me, that I have no more sense of my sins." These words were deliberately chosen to convey not a momentary but an abiding impression. The sentence immediately preceding is: "Very often, for these many years, these expressions are in my mind and in my mouth. — Infinite upon infinite, Infinite upon infinite."

These are not the utterances of a narrow soul, cramped and darkened by a morbid melancholy, but of a royal nature, grand in its perceptions and its emotions. While entertaining these views of sin, he was not despondent, but he could say: "Of late years I have had a more full and constant sense of the absolute sovereignty of God, and a delight in that sovereignty; and have had more of a sense of the glory of Christ, as a mediator revealed in the gospel. On one Saturday night in particular, I had such a discovery of the excellency of the gospel above all other doctrines, that I could not but say to myself, This is my chosen light, my chosen doctrine; and of Christ, This is my chosen Prophet. It appeared sweet, beyond all expression, to follow Christ, and to be taught and enlightened and instructed by Him; to learn of Him and live to Him. Another Saturday night (January, 1739, thirty-five years of age) I had such a sense how sweet and blessed a thing it was to walk in the way of duty, to do that which was right and meet to be done, and agreeable to the holy mind of God, that it caused me to break forth into a kind of loud weeping, which held me some time, so that I was forced to shut myself up and fasten the doors. I could not but, as it were, cry out, How happy are they which do that which is right in the sight of God! They are blessed indeed! they are the happy ones!"

Such a sense of sin as was habitual with this great and good man can be met by nothing less, nothing else, than "the glorious gospel of the ever blessed God." And such a sense may any man have if he possesses the requisite intelligence, and is enlightened by the Spirit of God. There is a Power working among men adequate to a similar result in the case of any competent, well-instructed mind. The Holy Ghost can sweep away the sophistries of men, so energize the conscience, and so reveal the glory of the Lord, that they shall cry ʻout, "Woe is me, I am undone!" "Behold, I am vile!" And the providence of God may put other thoughts into minds little accustomed to serious reflection. The voice which once shook the earth may also shake the heavens, and, by confusing the order of nature, confound the thoughts of the wise. Those who have been loudest in their eulogies of her may be most at their wits' end, when "there shall be signs in the sun, and in the moon, and in the stars, and upon the earth distress of nations; the sea and the waves roaring; men's hearts failing them for fear, and for looking after those things which are coming on the earth."

If a generation, wise in its own conceit, will not learn the fear of the Lord from the teachings of His word and the common works of His hand, there are wonders of counsel and might at His call. In any event, He will be exalted in the earth, and men shall acknowledge that He sitteth King for ever, enthroned high above all the works of His own hands, high over all the imaginations and doings of the children of pride. Shaken by His power, convicted by His Spirit, the boldest deniers of His presence and agency, the most complacent worshippers of nature and themselves, may be seized with a trembling like that of Belshazzar, when the fingers of a man's hand came forth to write upon the wall of his palace. No man can safely affirm that he is proof against an overwhelming sense of his sin against God, or secure from an overwhelming fear of His displeasure, unless he has laid hold of the hope set before him in the gospel. Before such a sense of sin, the doctrines of naturalism and the sacrifices of paganism flee away like chaff before the wind.

But supposing there were no such thing as sin, or fear, or wrath, still the soul of growing intelligence would need *love*, both subjective and objective, which can be found only in and through the gospel. This is the great radical want of every soul. And only that God, whose grace bringeth salvation, can either inspire in us, or bestow upon us, an adequate love. Admiration of the beautiful is not the same thing as love of the good; and, in order to be complete, we must do more than admire, — we must love. We may love an unworthy object inordinately;

but the power of loving cannot be fully developed without embracing a great and good object; cannot reach its highest without finding and resting upon the Greatest and the Best. Beyond all other objects ever known or conceived of, the creating, preserving, redeeming God of the Scriptures has power, and power because He has worth, to beget and develop love in the human soul. — a love true, pure, great, tender, active, enduring, eternal. In many ways is this worth displayed, this power exerted; but beyond and above all else in the redemption through Christ Jesus. Here, most emphatically, is the hiding of this power. There is nothing great enough and good enough for us to love with all the heart, but this God of grace. Naturalism, pantheism, may set before us marvels to excite our wonder and admiration, but they give us no such object to love.

On the other hand, there is no other such Being, no other being great and good enough to *love us* as we long to be loved. Precious, indeed, is the love of human hearts. But in feeling and purpose they come short of our necessities, especially when, by reflection and culture and divine teaching, we become conscious of the greatness of our need. We might be comfortable, possibly content, with nothing higher or stronger than the devoted attachment of pure unselfish human hearts, but our joy could not be full. Room has God made in these hearts for His own infinite love, and room that never can be *filled* by any thing else. The language of the man who has become conscious of his need is: "As the hart panteth after the water-brooks, so panteth my soul after thee, O God. My soul thirsteth for God, for the living God." And the language of one who has found the supply is: "Whom have I in heaven but thee? and there is none upon earth that I desire besides thee. . . . God is the strength of my heart, and my portion for ever."

Impersonal nature, however great and varied her charms, cannot give us love. This greatest, most enduring want of the soul can be met, is met, and we have abundant reason to believe will be met for ever, by the Father of our spirits and the Saviour of our souls. "Herein is love, not that we loved God, but that he loved us, and sent his Son to be the propitiation for our sins." "And we have known and believed the love that God hath to us. God is love; and he that dwelleth in love dwelleth in God, and God in him."

Thus being loved, and loving thus, we must be supremely and for ever blessed. To a soul thus developed, ennobled, satisfied, what are the trials incident to this mortal life? Those who can say, "The love of God is shed abroad in our hearts by the Holy Ghost which is given unto us," can also add, "We rejoice in hope of the glory of God; we glory in tribulation also, knowing that tribulation worketh patience, and patience experience, and experience hope, and hope maketh not ashamed." And may we not confidently affirm that this love creates a better atmosphere for the cure, the comfort, and the true development of our poor stricken humanity, than that which surrounds the purest philosophers and the noblest teachers of science, who have learned nothing in the school of Christ? What else can so soften, refine, adorn, and ennoble the nature made rugged and selfish by indwelling sin, and made bitter and reckless by the wrongs inflicted upon it? Knowledge we do not despise; but love, God's own to us, and such in us for God and man as the gospel alone can inspire, we *must* have, to smooth the rugged way of life, and fit us for our mission to our kind. In this atmosphere we would live and die, and live again, and live for ever.

X.

GRANDEUR OF ITS PRACTICAL MISSION.

THE *gospel work is one to invite and engross the very best powers of our minds and our hearts.* It should be reckoned a privilege and not a burden. We naturally thirst for something to do. Indolence has indeed been spoken of facetiously as "our original sin." And there is a coloring of truth in the representation. And yet the common aversion to work is not an indisposition toward all activity, but only toward certain forms of it. The little child is not simply restless, but eager also to do something. That something may not be useful, but it requires the exercise of strength, calculation, and perhaps all the little stock of knowledge as yet possessed. It would probably be as correct to say that men acquire as to say that they inherit idle tendencies. And never can a man be fully satisfied with himself without employing his faculties and energies in some useful calling. It is not really a question with us whether we shall be active or inactive, so long as we are able to accomplish any thing either with our brains or with our hands. We are impelled by an inward, if not an outward, necessity to be doing something daily. The impulse is not indeed sufficient with all, for the doing of any thing like what they are capable of. But if those comparatively idle are satisfied with themselves, their course does not commend itself to any earnest, noble mind. It is barely possible that a man may be so indolent, that he cannot even appreciate the schemes and achievements of more earnest men. But, ordinarily, those least efficient are ready to praise the man of lofty ambition and heroic labors. And sometimes, by such examples, the idle are made ashamed of their aimless and useless lives.

It being settled, then, that we are to do something, are to employ our energies upon some kind of business, the question arises, How may they be employed in the most worthy, useful, and satisfying manner? The work now under consideration furnishes the best answer to this question. Here is a mission, whose tendencies are unmistakably good, — more than this, are the best conceivable, — and whose measure gives scope for all the faculties and energies of any and every man. The tendencies are so obvious, and so well understood in a Christian community, that there is no occasion to dwell upon them here. True gospel work embraces every right form of teaching, healing, purifying, elevating, strengthening, enriching, and comforting ministration. Its aim is to form a perfect character, fill the mind with the knowledge of the greatest things, and the heart with the purest and sublimest joys. In connection with this, it favors such alleviations of the ills, and such enhancement of the benefits, pertaining to the outward estate, as the highest wellbeing of the individual and of society may require. To the work of the gospel, carried out according to the plan and in the spirit of its great Author, no candid, truth-loving, and benevolent mind can object. No man can possibly desire to do any thing better for his fellowmen, any thing which will more certainly secure and increase their moral worth, or redound more to their lasting happiness. The kind of work, taken in a comprehensive sense, is just what an enlightened reason and a pure heart must judge most fit and needful to be done.

But this work is great as well as good. And by this characteristic, it is in a special manner commended to an enlightened mind. With the progress of knowledge, in science and art, men are learning to do *great* things; *i.e.*, things which are great in comparison with the achievements, or even the ideas, of an earlier age. They project and accomplish gigantic schemes. They make highways for thought under the ocean, for trade and travel across the continents. They amass splendid fortunes, and rear magnificent palaces. They are moving toward the recognition of all nations as members of one great family, with common interests, and made for mutual acquaintance and profit.

They are looking to the ends of the earth in their calculations for gain or pleasure. Not a few despise small plans, and are impatient of slow gains. They are for a larger place and bolder operations than those which satisfied their fathers.

And not in material enterprises alone are men making themselves familiar with broad plans and great endeavors. In the domain of knowledge they are pushing their discoveries into the depths below and the heights above, laying bare secrets of the ocean, and uncovering the face of stars, which have been hid from the foundation of the world. In ethics and politics and social relations, they are agitating, if not compassing, great revolutions. These things all spring from a growing intelligence, although some of their experiments may be little to its credit. But however crude some of the theories, or harmful even some of the expedients, which are born of this mental quickening, they foster a passion for schemes of amazing magnitude and splendor. It is requisite, therefore, if a moral undertaking is to hold its own, and win new victories, in such an age, that it should have a vastness in keeping with these schemes of secular wisdom and enterprise, or far outreaching them all.

And this is the character of the Christian enterprise, considered as an agency for effecting changes in the character and fortunes of mankind. Its grandeur is made evident when we consider the *material* which it takes in hand, the *forces* by which it shapes this material to its purpose, the *excellence* of the perfected *result*, and the *extent* of its actual or intended operations.

What is the material in hand? It is the human soul, or man as a moral being, — intelligent, responsible, immortal. The business of Christianity, specifically, is to transform this being into the likeness of God, and set him in relations of fellowship and co-operation with God. Of the value of this soul, no adequate estimate can be formed by any mind which cannot fathom infinity and eternity. The impressive, the startling words of our Saviour, " What shall it profit a man if he shall gain the whole world, and lose his own soul?" fail to convey to us any thing like a full, an exhaustive idea of its priceless worth. How high, comparatively, does the rational being stand on the scale of created objects? At the head of this lower and visible creation, and but a little below the angels, is this creature man. And above the angels we know of none but God. And, indeed, we are told that "God created man in his own image." Reason, imagination, judgment, conscience, will, what faculties are these! To what a development of strength, order, and beauty they may be brought! The desires, the aspirations, the passions, the affections, what powers are these! To what degradation and shame they may sink, or to what dignity and glory they may lift, the soul! What susceptibilities, what capabilities, in this creature man! Shut up to this little corner of the universe, made the tenant of a frail earthly tabernacle, compassed about with infirmities, he can nevertheless send his thoughts backward far beyond the beginning of measured time, and onward far beyond the point at which time shall be no longer, and outward beyond the orbits of uncounted and invisible worlds, and upward to the very throne of the eternal God. He can frame instruments, by which he may bring to light the hidden things of darkness, searching with equal ease the microscopic and the telescopic spheres, and making real to his apprehension in these domains an infinitude of things small and great.

And these magnificent capabilities may all be used in quick response to the mandates of the eternal King, with the conscious and the willing purpose to glorify Him, and further the great ends by Him ordained. The laws of nature are beautiful in their simplicity, order, and majesty, but they have neither consciousness nor volition. The instincts of animals are often charming in their accuracy, strength, and utility,—their affections, also, in their tenderness and fitness,—but they cannot entertain a moral purpose, nor perform a moral action. Here man stands alone, or with the angels and with God. Oh that in the best sense it could be said that here he *stands!* But, alas! he has fallen by his iniquity; and yet, in his fall, has not made his soul less precious. Lost in a spiritual sense, and most unworthy, and yet in God's thought too precious to be lost, without any and every practicable sacrifice to redeem it! The recovery of this soul, whose redemption is so precious, is the work of the gospel. Is there any other work like it? Should some evil power quench the light and destroy the heat of the sun, so that the earth and all the other planets would roll around it in darkness, desolation, and death, and then a good spirit should rekindle its fires, and so bring back to us the old brightness, beauty, and life, he would be a benefactor worthy of unmeasured praise, and yet less a benefactor than this gospel, which brings life and immortality to light; which lays hold of dead souls, and wakes them to newness of life; which brings these wandering stars, that were on their way to the blackness of darkness for ever, back to their place, and pours upon them the effulgence of the Sun of righteousness.

And by what forces does the gospel shape this

precious soul into the likeness of God? The purest and the richest of which we have any knowledge, or of which we are able to conceive, — the attractions of love, human and divine love. "The Spirit and the bride say, Come." A word first about the office of human love. Men are employed as instruments in persuading their fellow-men to receive the gospel. And if they expect any success in this work, they must speak the truth in love. This has been exemplified in the history of many successful workers in the vineyard of the Lord. Take one example, that of the apostle Paul. Such love had he for his people that he said, "I could wish that myself were accursed from Christ for my brethren, my kinsmen according to the flesh." And this was his way of pleading with men to receive the gospel: "Now, then, we are ambassadors for Christ, as though God did beseech you by us: we pray you in Christ's stead, be ye reconciled to God." This love for souls, which is born of love to God, is the purest and the strongest which man bears toward his fellow-man. The love of husbands and wives, of parents and children, is often extremely tender and beautiful. But, to this, additional charms and strength are imparted by a true apprehension of the worth of the soul, and a Christian concern for its salvation.

And even where there are no ties of kindred, or interest, or friendship, in the common acceptation of that term, this gospel love is often a consuming passion. It is benevolence quickened and intensified by the fear that souls will perish, by a dread for them of everlasting burnings, and by the anticipation of their unending felicity. How can we possibly exert our influence so well as through this affection of grace? What are personal charms, or learning, or wealth, or position, as means of influence, compared with this undying, unselfish, unspeakable love of souls? And we are not to reckon this kind of human love as unworthy of a place in this great work of drawing men to goodness and to God. Even divine love, that it might be made most efficient, became allied with the human. Christ loved as a man not less truly than as God. In that tearful lament over Jerusalem, we perceive the yearning of human as well as divine compassion. By His lifting up does He draw all men to Him. And God is in Christ reconciling the world unto Himself.

And when we come to speak of divine love, in distinction from human, we can only *touch* an ocean without bottom and without shore. Here is all the fulness of God, for God is love. The ways in which this love are expressed are countless, and many of them amazing. The bounties and the charms of nature declare it; the care of daily providence confirms it; the facts, ordinances, and promises of revelation magnify it; and the history of grace through all the weary ages illustrates it. In no one of these departments can we measure its fulness. The world around us and the heavens above us are crowded with the shining tokens of God's wisdom and beneficence, of His care for our sustenance and our enjoyment. The history of every day is replete with evidence that " His tender mercies are over all His works." But more especially in the gospel of His grace is this love made known. Here come to view the length, the breadth, the depth, and the height, in each of which it passeth knowledge.

The commandment which meets us here is holy, just, and good. The types and shadows of the earlier dispensation are full of pleasing intimations of the grace to be revealed. And the coming of the great Deliverer was such an unspeakable boon, that prophets must be commissioned, in a long line of succession, to predict it, and angels charged to appear in hosts to celebrate it. And the Spirit of inspiration, who searcheth all things, yea, the deep things of God, and who is also the Spirit of truth, proclaims: "In this was manifested the love of God toward us, because that God sent his only begotten Son into the world, that we might live through him." Many times and in many forms is this repeated in the true sayings of God. This is the sum of the good tidings of great joy. And the Spirit is ready to make this message of grace effectual to the salvation of all them that believe. The demonstration and the application are both of God. Here we behold the Father giving, the Son dying, the Spirit revealing, Each and All intent upon our redemption. The cross is the consecrated sign, and the church the enduring monument, of this eternal love of the triune God. With the cords of this love does He draw and bind men to Himself. And in this work He grants us also a share; putting it upon us, if we will consent, to make known the exceeding riches of His grace, and to exhibit in the purity and blessedness of our own lives the benign efficacy of His transforming power. Can we elsewhere wield so choice and potent an influence as this? Looking at this kind of power, and considering wherein its glory lies, noting the disposition in which it began, the purpose by which it was disclosed, the sacrifice by which it was proved, and the way in which it is applied, can we not see that there is no honor like that of being "laborers together with God"?

But we must pass on to look at the perfected result of this gospel work. At every stage it is a good work, but it cannot be fully understood until it is finished. In one sense it is finished when the work of sanctification is complete, when every thought of the renewed man has been brought into captivity to Christ. We are permitted to see some examples, in which this work seems to be nearly or quite complete. And we must confess that a perfect "Christian is the highest style of man." And the highest style of man is the *best* thing upon the earth. A Christian is not perfect until the same mind is in him that is in Christ, — the same not only in its general spirit and purpose, but also in all subordinate particulars so far as we may have the mind of Christ. He must be a singular man, or a reckless one, who, with the Gospels in his hand, can fail to see and confess that in Christ our humanity finds its completeness and crown. That is a distempered fancy, which dreams of going beyond and improving upon this model of all excellence. No man, with a decent regard for truth, has ventured to say that He does not hold a very lofty place. Even the followers of Mohammed allow this. And few, if any, will be found to deny that it would be an infinite advantage if the world generally could be brought up to this high standard, an immense advantage to any community which can be named, however select, enlightened, advanced. And, without a question, it will be discovered that any who think they are going beyond are really falling behind. This is *just* what man needs, — no less, no more, — to reach the measure of the stature of the fulness of Christ. And if this is the point of perfection, then it must be a good thing, the best thing practicable, to be pressing ourselves and drawing others, with all our might, toward it. What we do at any particular time is to be estimated with reference to the completeness toward which it is reaching. And it is matter for devout thankfulness and rejoicing, that He who hath begun a good work in us or others will carry it on unto perfection. There is no reason to fear that we shall lose our labor, when it is expended upon new-born souls. The earlier parts of the work are not less essential than the later, which may seem more excellent. He that soweth and he that reapeth may rejoice together.

Individual perfection, great and desirable as

it is, cannot show all the strength and beauty of gospel work. This takes account of man as a social being, and aims not only to make him worthy of his place in the family, in society, in the church, and in the state, but also to make all these worthy of him. And, obviously, in proportion as individuals are perfected, the associations of them, whether larger or smaller, will become so also. But organizations, however faultless in theory, will be imperfect in practice, while the individuals composing them are imperfect. The true method of securing the completeness of society, in all its forms, or that upon which the *chief* reliance should be placed, is by pressing individuals closer and closer to the great standard of righteousness. When there is no wrong in individuals, there can be none in society. And when the preponderance in any association or community is decidedly in favor of the righteous, it will be an easy thing to bring institutions, customs, and laws, to the most desirable form, and work them with the requisite efficiency. And, indeed, we might almost say that in this condition of the body, — domestic, social, or politic, — these things will regulate themselves, so spontaneous and powerful will be the general impulse to shape, preserve, and use them, according to the rights and needs of all parties in interest.

But the perfected man and perfected society, as they are or may be seen upon this earthly theatre of action, disclose only the beginning of the grand result at which the gospel aims. These are introductory: the great life, the great joys, belong to the future, the eternal state. This is the crowning glory of gospel work, that it is for ever. The choicest works of human genius, which are of the earth earthy, must in time feel the touch of decay; must, at least, share in the destructive changes to which the earth itself is reserved. But this work of grace, wrought in deathless souls, will change only from glory to glory. The risen body, incorruptible and immortal, joined with the glorified spirit, sinless and raised above every weakness, these in exact harmony, and in the presence of God and the Lamb! — what higher, what better, what fuller, can there be than this? What more is there to contemplate or receive, except the multiplying of the numbers by whom this fulness is enjoyed? And this idea of numbers brings us to the remaining thought named, as indicating the true character and grandeur of the gospel work. A scheme so high in its origin, so peculiar and wonderful in its development, so noble in its purpose, so rich in its provisions, so genial in its spirit, so attractive in its forces, and so benignant in its operation, must be fitted, and, we should say, also designed, for a prevalence in proportion to its excellence. And if we ask the great Author concerning His purpose, He declares to us that "the field is the world," and the day of its power is until the end of the world. He solemnly charges us to "go into all the world, and preach the gospel to every creature." There is no place for halting, until the earth shall be full of the knowledge of the Lord. We are not allowed to overlook either the near or the remote. The first apostles, whose commission covered all nations, must begin at Jerusalem. Those who had high thoughts of the kingdom must not despise any little one. In this comprehensiveness of design, the gospel is like the creating wisdom of God. The little insect — too small for our unaided vision, too feeble for our care — has received from the divine Hand as perfect a finish, and from the divine resources as perfect a provision, as ourselves, or as any brightest orb or angel in the heights of heaven. The gospel is for man, in a very important sense for man only; but it is for universal man. And the business of those called into the vineyard of the Lord is to give free course to the gospel in all lands, as quickly as possible, by all the facilities at their command for so high and spiritual a purpose. In Christian communities, in a large number of Christian families, new subjects are coming forward to be moulded by its spirit, or to go out and wield their influence against it. In the church itself are some to be reclaimed from their wanderings, many to be urged onward and upward to higher attainments in grace, and nobler achievements for Christ.

Some have a name to live, and lo! they are dead. To these, of whatever name, — Greek, Roman, Armenian, or Nestorian, — the gospel is to be brought as a quickening power. And in the regions beyond, millions rise upon millions, who have not yet heard the precious Name. They have their own religions, but in them is but little to guide, purify, or comfort, nothing to save, their souls. They are wedded to their superstitions, and may think themselves wiser than those who come to show them the way of life.

And some there are, who would leave them under their delusions, because, in their view, these, if not the best things, are at least well enough for them. They even account it a reproach to Christianity, that it aims to supersede all these, because, as it alleges, they cannot save the soul. They esteem it intolerance in the advocates of the gospel, if not also in its Author, that they allow no other foundation for human hope. Nothing is plainer than this, that Christ, in His own apprehension, came not to be a king among kings, a lord among lords, but the King of kings and Lord of lords. There is a sense in which the gospel is uncompromising, full as it is of all sweetest tenderness and gentle charities. It claims the whole world, because it is the word of the *one only*, the living, and the true God, to the creatures whom He alone has made, and whom alone His only Son can redeem. It claims the whole world, because it speaks in the name of the one great Sovereign of the world. Christ claims the faith and obedience of all men, because He came down from heaven, and gave Himself a ransom for all.

Lords many and gods many there may be in the faiths of fallen men, and these may have their rivalries, but He who made the heavens and the earth acknowledges none of them. Knowing that there is no God except Himself, it is His right to require that men shall not acknowledge any other. Christ, the only real incarnation of God, may justly claim the homage of all for whom He became flesh, and for whom in the flesh He laid down His life. To do otherwise would be to deny Himself, to bring Himself down to a level with the creations of men. While He rejects nothing that is true and good in the teachings of any man, He claims to be "the Way, the Truth, and the Life."

Confucius, Gautama, Zoroaster, Mohammed, and many others revered by multitudes as sources of divine knowledge, taught much truth; but not one of them is a Saviour, not one of them is King of truth. When the gospel comes to their adherents, it does not require them to renounce any true doctrine, or abandon any right practice. And yet, without a question, their systems of faith and worship as such will be overturned by the gospel, wherever it is received. And what harm, we may here inquire, if all these systems should give place to the gospel? Are they doing such great things for their adherents, that these would suffer loss if they should be taken away, and Christianity installed in their stead? This question may be answered by asking two more. Where are the nations to-day, that cling to any of these systems, and yet are in advance of the great

Christian nations, or that ever were in advance of them, with respect to culture, character, institutions, and the means for obtaining and dispensing either the common comforts or the choicest enjoyments of life? And what is the character of the work wrought by the heralds of the cross in our times among the adherents of these systems, so far as they have been able to prevail with them to receive the gospel? Have they not been lifted to a higher plane of intelligence, civilization, morals, and enjoyment?

But even if the objections, which some urge against what they call the exclusiveness or intolerance of Christianity, were valid, little would be taken from the sublimity of the mission to which it calls its adherents. With reason or without reason, Christ summons His followers to attempt the conversion of the world. And they who truly believe in Him cannot set any narrower limits to their commission. And if they are true to their own faith, they will throw themselves into this great undertaking. And there is nothing so sublime in human action as this. It would be a grand scheme to convert a single race, or some great empire like that of China or Japan. But it is far grander to embrace all races, all empires, all tribes; all kindred, and all tongues.

But the bare naming of the countries and the peoples, the survey of the vast area for which the gospel is designed, does not convey any thing like an adequate idea of the work to be accomplished. It would be no very difficult thing to raise an army of heralds, and send them forth into all lands. It would be no special burden for these heralds to deliver their message, if the nations were only waiting to receive them. But the way must be prepared. A language unformed must be reduced to order; another, bristling all over with difficulties, must be acquired, and when acquired, found deficient in terms to state the cardinal truths of the gospel; prejudices must be removed, hostility abated, hypocrisy circumvented, and all the twistings and turnings of human perversity followed and defeated. It is especially in this variety, fulness, complexity, and obstinacy of the details, which confront the great enterprise, that we see the loftiness of aim and purpose which moved Him, who first undertook Himself and now summons us to such a service, and which must move those who would enter heartily and efficiently into it. He who gets his eye fairly upon this work, and his heart and hands fully in it, will not be in want of a mission to engross his sympathies or employ his energies. He will not ask for any thing greater, but only for wisdom, grace, and strength, to make full proof of his ministry. The names of Alexander and Cæsar will be kept, not only in the knowledge, but also in the admiration of multitudes, perhaps as long as the world shall stand, because in their daring ambition they conquered the world. But the glory of the Macedonian and of the Roman is a poor and hollow thing in comparison with that which shall accrue to the Captain of our salvation, when great voices in heaven shall proclaim that "the kingdoms of this world are become the kingdoms of our Lord, and of his Christ; and he shall reign for ever and ever."

And in that glory shall every man have a share, if only he has been a faithful helper unto the kingdom of God. The service is one, in whatever age, country, or sphere performed. The poor widow, who cast her two mites into the treasury of the Lord, will have a part in the honor of the final triumph as surely as that great apostle, who, from Jerusalem round about unto Illyricum, fully preached the gospel of Christ. There is no right and worthy thing to be done, which may not be made a part of this service. Every man in his own calling, in his own place and business, provided they are such as God can approve, may bear a part in pressing forward the standards of the conquering host.

And this is a thing of the greatest moment. If nothing could be done in this great enterprise except in particular lines of effort, — like making a pilgrimage, or preaching the word in the way of set and official discourse, — only a few could have a part in it. The necessities of life bind most to other kinds of service. Christ is not unmindful of these necessities.

His regard for them is evinced by that saying, "The sabbath was made for man, not man for the sabbath." Some parts of human care and toil seem to have little dignity or use, as compared with others; but we should remember that what is feeble may be even more necessary. Great trusts are few, and but few are called to meet them. Little things are many, and to the many it is given to do them. If one desires the office of a bishop, he desires a good work. But one may also receive the reward of a good and faithful servant, if, whatever little things he is called to do, he does them heartily as unto the Lord. Every kind of lawful and useful business should be regarded and followed as a divinely appointed stewardship.

The fault of many is not in what they do, but in doing it for themselves outside of the vineyard of the Lord. We can do the most common things out of respect to the will of God, and with the abiding purpose to honor Him. We can hold our time, our plans, our activities, our pleasures, and our gains, at God's bidding and disposal. So doing, we shall be in His service, let our calling be what it may. To suffer for Christ's sake belongs also to this comprehensive service. And in the grand economy of grace, perhaps, none can so ill be spared as those who suffer for Him. The finer and more difficult parts of the work are given to them. And those who are too poor to give, too weak to labor, and so mercifully cared for that they need not suffer, may with their praying breath help on the great endeavor. With a look of sympathy, and a word of supplication and of benediction, the dying may hallow it and give it impulse. And if one has genius to devise and strength to execute great things, he will find room in this service for the best he can think or say or do. The difficulty of explaining and applying the word of God so as to reach the minds and hearts of young and old, of them that are near and them afar off, of defending the faith against the assaults of impiety and unbelief, of projecting and working necessary agencies for the relief of suffering and the supply of want, will so tax his wisdom and his endurance, that he will be constrained to say, "Who is sufficient for these things?" Entering fully into the work of Christ, he will find it broad and deep and high enough for all the wisdom of men, taught and strengthened by the wisdom of God.

XI.

CONCLUSION.

SOME claiming to be the most advanced thinkers of this age do not scruple to set aside the gospel as effete, or of less importance than the speculations and discoveries of their fertile minds. This assumption should lead all true believers to contend more earnestly for the faith once delivered to the saints. We will not disparage their persons or their acquisitions. But when Henry Buckle tells us, that " it may well be, that in the march of ages every definite and written creed now existing is to die out, and to be succeeded by better ones," our answer is, or would be, had he not already proved its truth in part, "All flesh is grass, and all the goodliness thereof is as the flower of the field. . . . The grass withereth, the flower fadeth: but the word of our God shall stand for ever." When John Stuart Mill says to us: "Many essential elements of the highest morality are not provided for, nor intended to be provided for, in the recorded deliverances of the Founder of Christianity. . . . I think it a great error to persist in attempting to find in the Christian doctrine that complete rule for our guidance, which its Author intended to enforce, but only partially to provide," our answer is: "The law of the Lord is perfect, converting the soul: the testimony of the Lord is sure, making wise the simple." "Though we, or an angel from heaven, preach any other gospel unto you than that which we have preached unto you, let him be accursed." When E. L. Youmans teaches us that "it is now established that the dependence of thought upon organic conditions is so intimate and absolute, that they can no longer be considered except as unity," we confront him with the words of the Royal Preacher: "Then shall the dust return to the earth as it was: and the spirit shall return unto God who gave it."

And when he further affirms: "The full-orbed intellect is yet to come, and will doubtless bring with it the perpetual motion and the Jews' Messias," we tell him that "grace and truth came by Jesus Christ;" that "God hath in these last days spoken unto us by his Son, . . . the brightness of his glory, and the express image of his person."

These men, and others like them, speaking in the name of History, Philosophy, and Science, have power to mislead many who have not known by experience the grace of our Lord Jesus Christ, and to unsettle the faith of some who have believed. Of all such, in so far as they make war upon Christianity, must we be able to say to those imperilled by their show of superior wisdom: "To whom we gave place by subjection, no, not for an hour; that the truth of the gospel may continue with you." Bold as is the tone of modern Unbelief, we have no occasion to be disquieted for the ark of God. The power of the Cross is mighty, our enemies themselves being judges. Lecky, in his laudation of Rationalism, makes this admission:

"When we look back to the cheerful alacrity with which, in some former ages, men sacrificed all their material and intellectual interests to what they believed to be right, and when we realize the unclouded assurance that was their reward, it is impossible to deny that we have lost something in our progress." Guizot tells us of an intelligent and distinguished disciple of Voltaire, who said to him: "It is not on my own account that I regret these attacks, but I ask for regularity and peace in my own household; I felicitate myself that my wife is a Christian, and I mean my daughters to be brought up like Christian women. These demolishers know not what they are doing; it is not merely upon our churches, it is upon our houses and their inmates, that their blows are telling!" And the philosopher Diderot is reported to have said to his associates, at the house of Baron d'Holbach: "In spite of all the evil we have spoken, and doubtless with reason enough, of this book, I defy you, with all your power, to compose a narrative which shall be as simple, but at the same time as sublime and as touching, as the recital of the passion and death of Jesus Christ; which shall produce the same effect, and make so strong a sensation, felt so generally by all, and the influence of which shall continue the same after so many ages." Astonishment and silence were the fit, the impressive, and the only answer.

Cambridge: Stereotyped and Printed by John Wilson and Son.

www.ingramcontent.com/pod-product-compliance
Lightning Source LLC
Chambersburg PA
CBHW020108170426
43199CB00009B/440